Camille Pissarro

Paintings

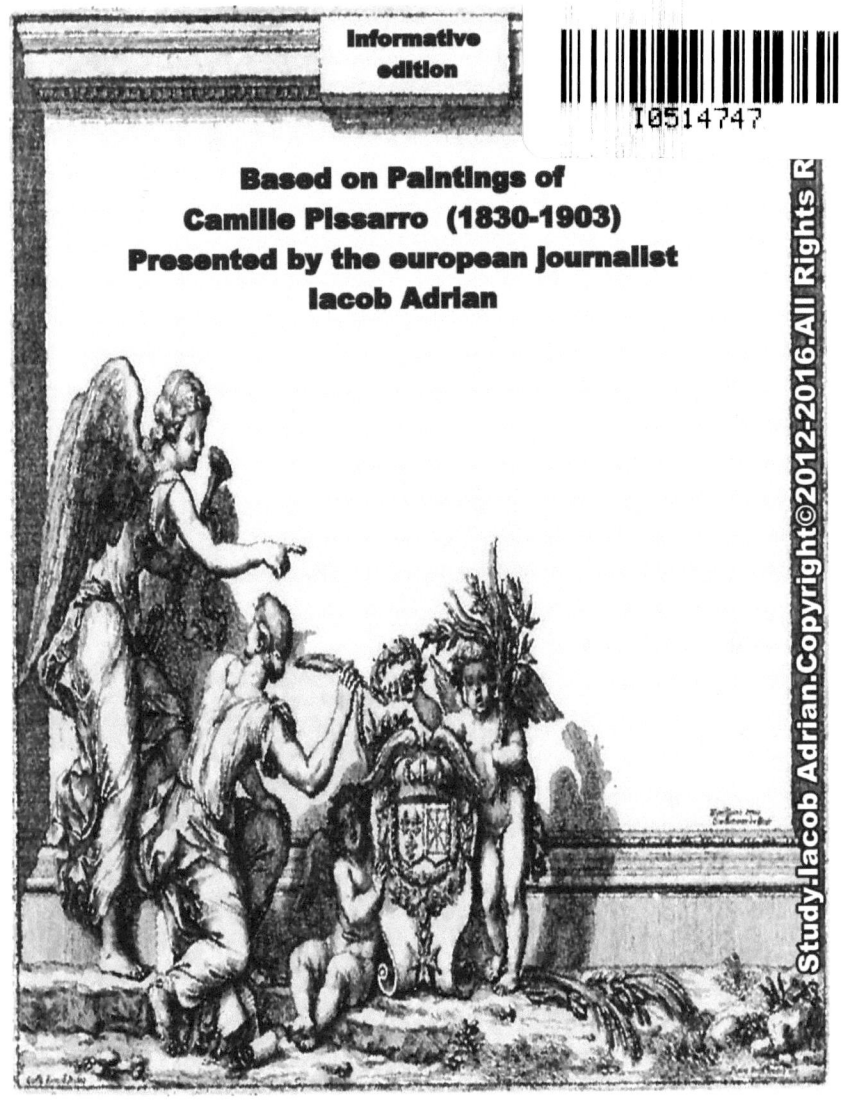

Informative edition

Based on Paintings of
Camille Pissarro (1830-1903)
Presented by the european journalist
Iacob Adrian

ISBN-13 : 978-1974615353 -- ISBN-10 : 1974615359

Notice

This documentary study use historic, archived documents. Because of this, some pages may look blurry or low quality. Still are included in this book because they have high value from critical, documentary, historical, informative and journalistic point of view .

Dtp and visual art
Iacob Adrian

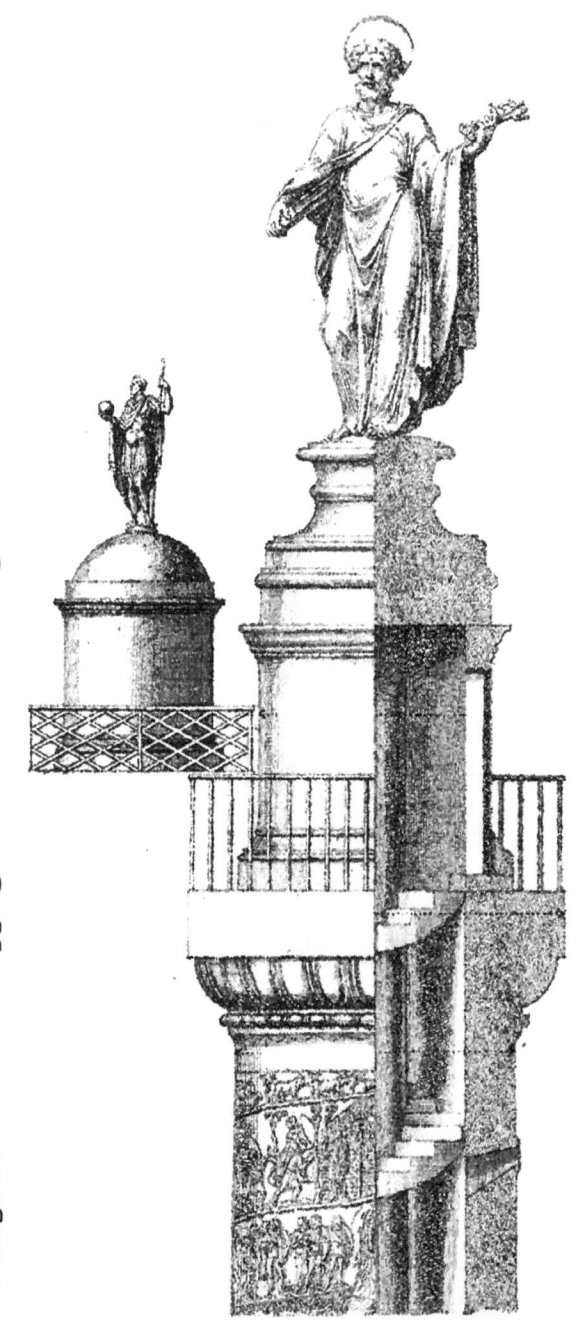

Editor
Iacob Adrian

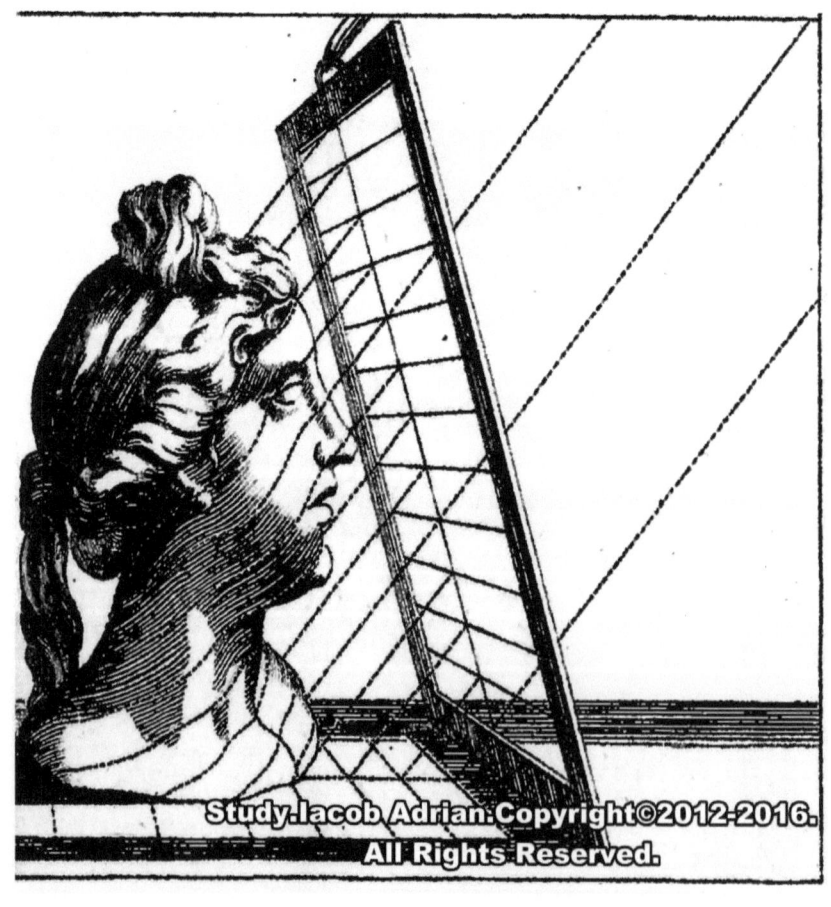

Editor statement

This is a series of classic books from classical authors .

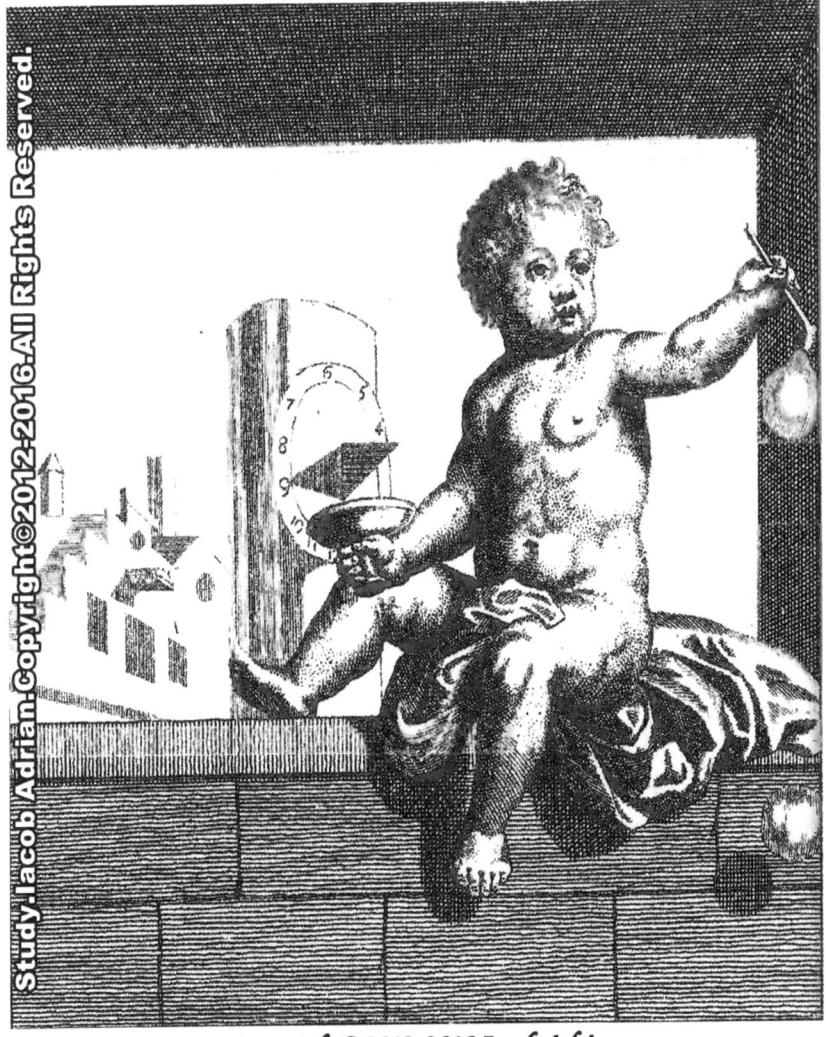

Copyright©2012-2016 Iacob Adrian
All Rights Reserved.

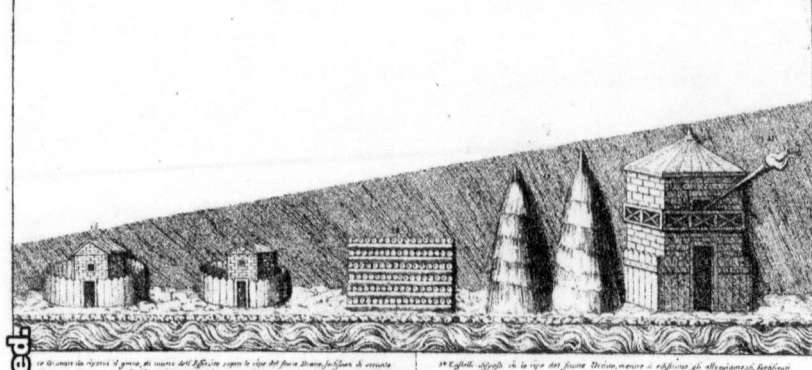

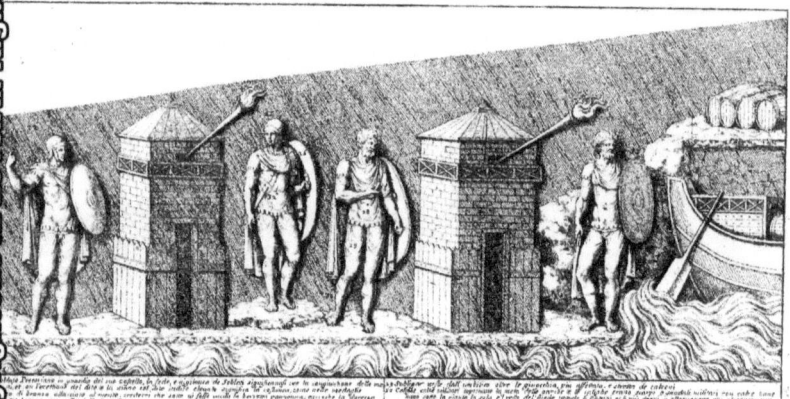

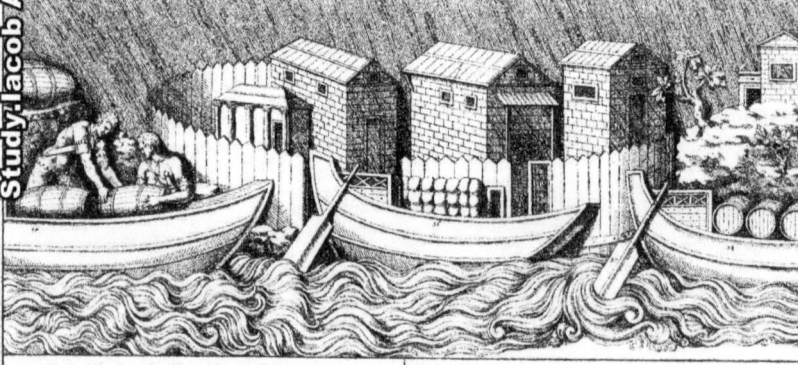

This little Book conveys the greetings of

....

to

....

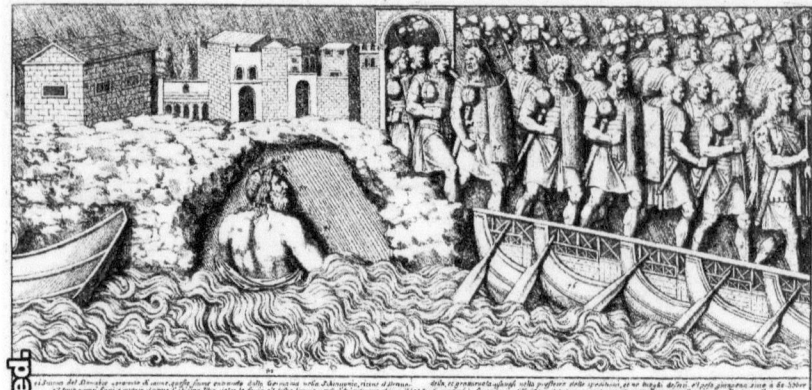

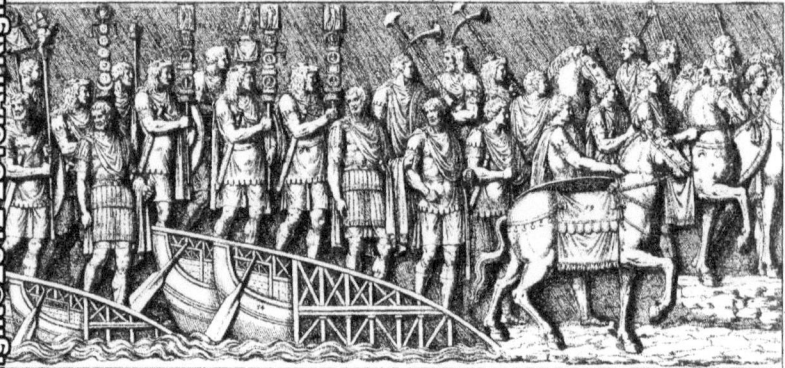

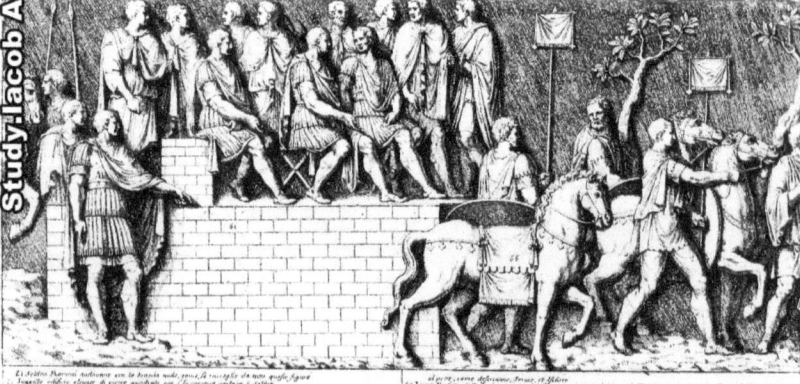

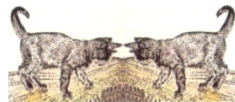

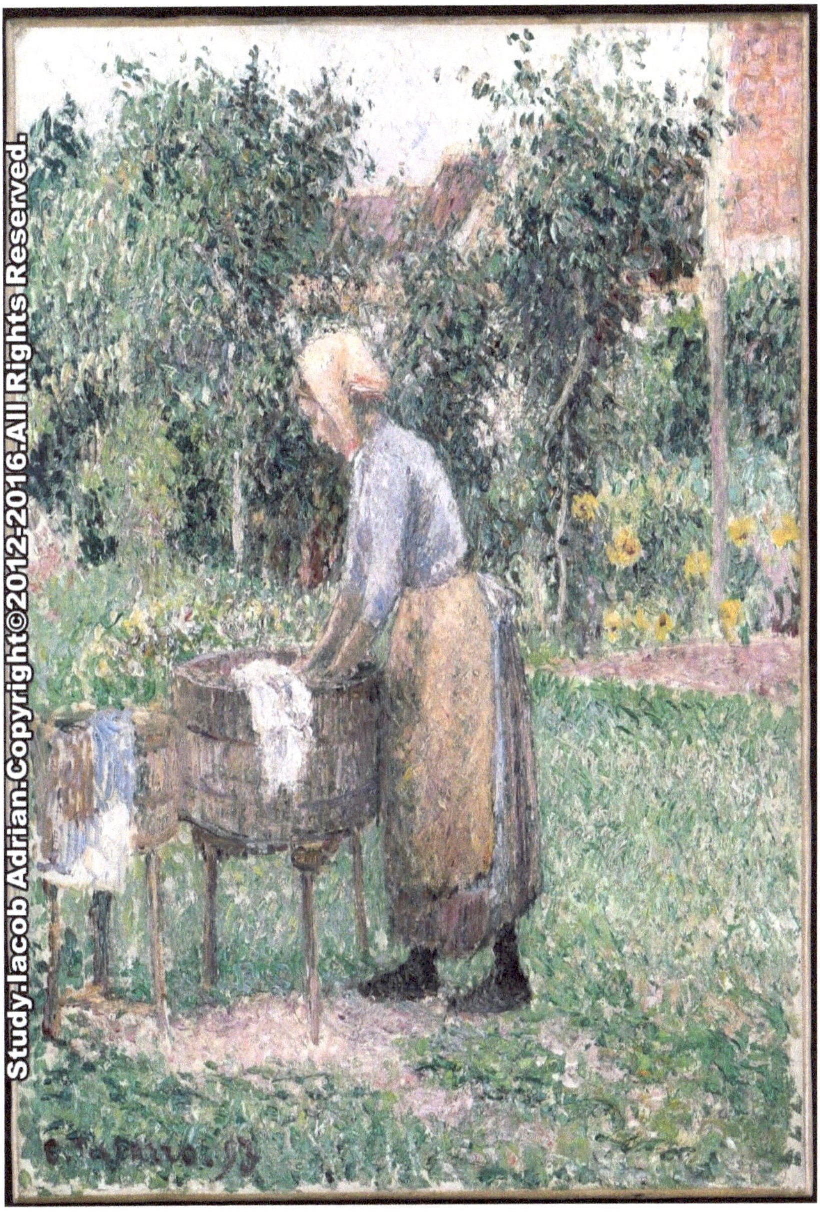

A Washerwoman at Éragny
Date : 1893

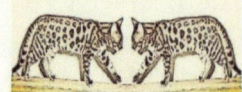

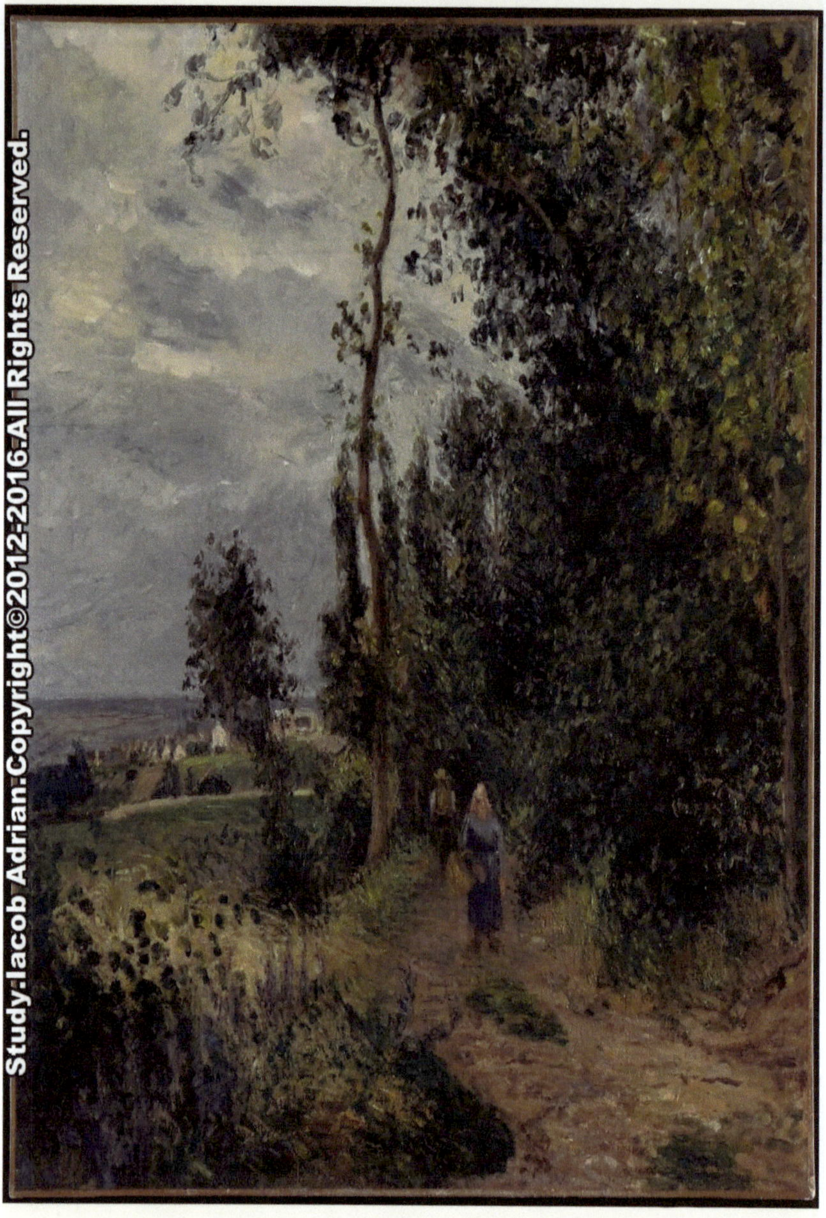

Côte des Grouettes, near Pontoise
Date : circa 1878

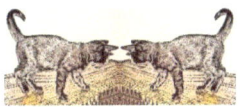

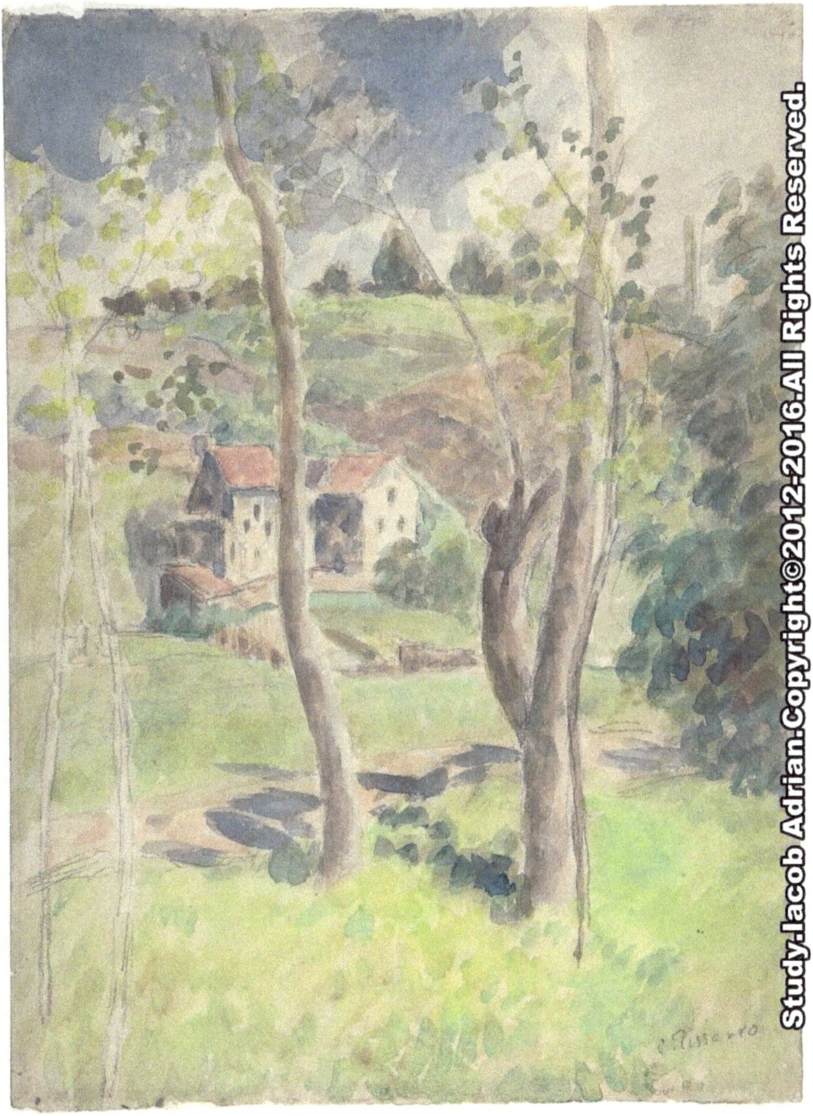

Landscape
Date : second half 19th century

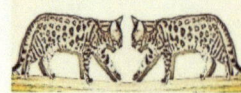

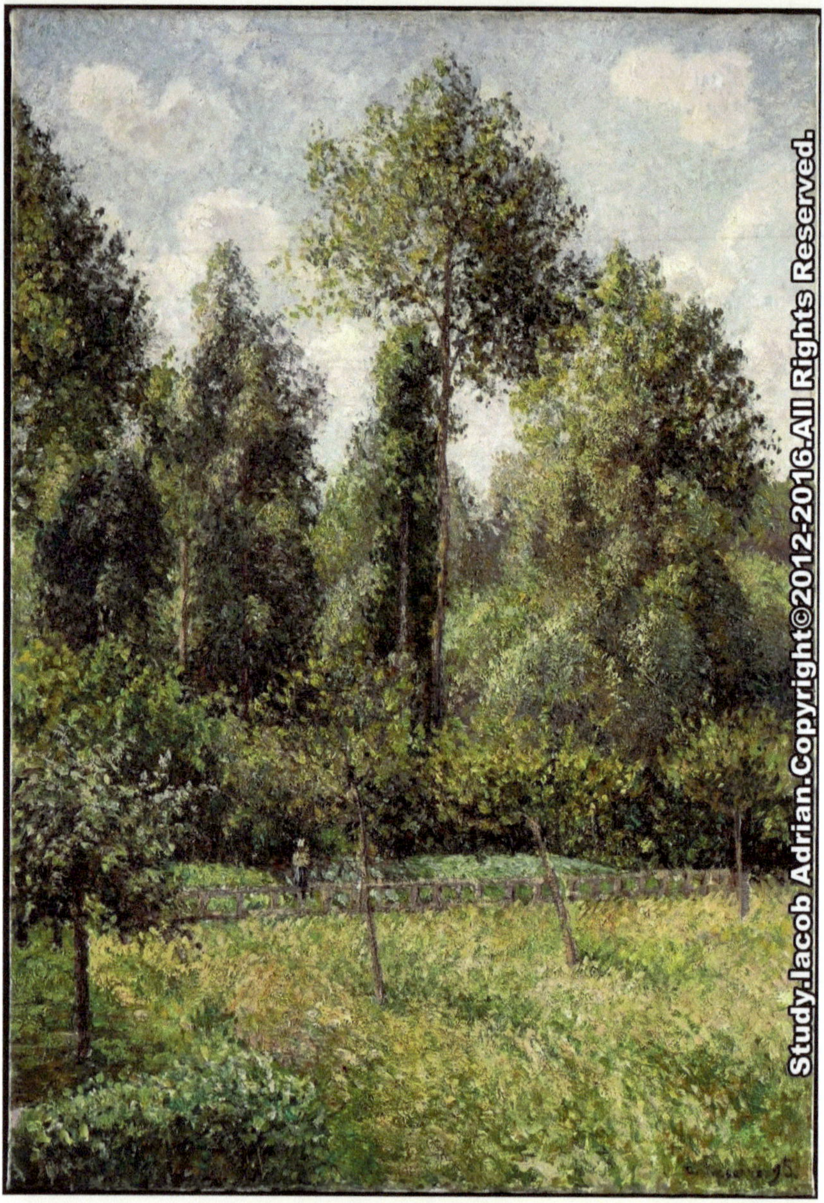

Poplars, Éragny
Date : 1895

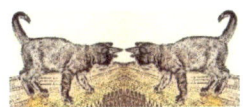

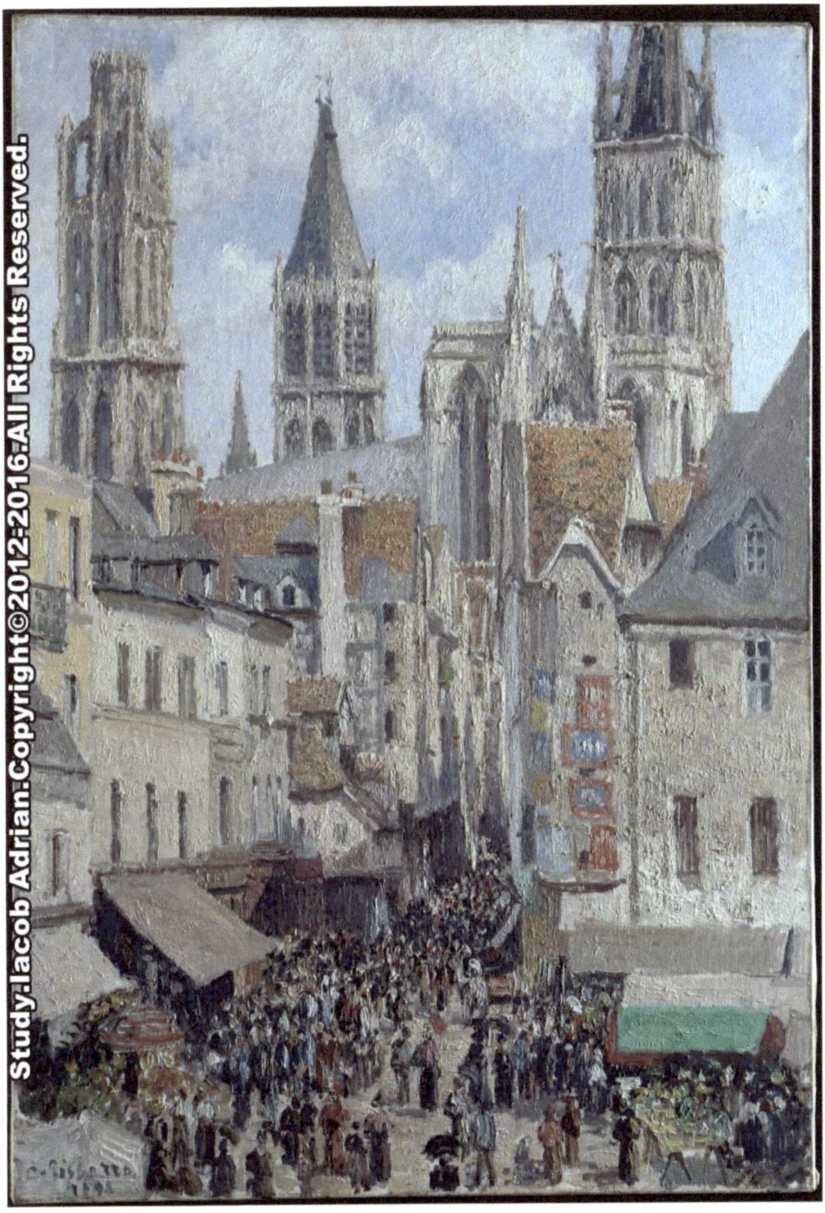

Rue de l'Épicerie, Rouen (Effect of Sunlight)
Date : 1898

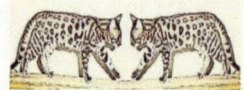

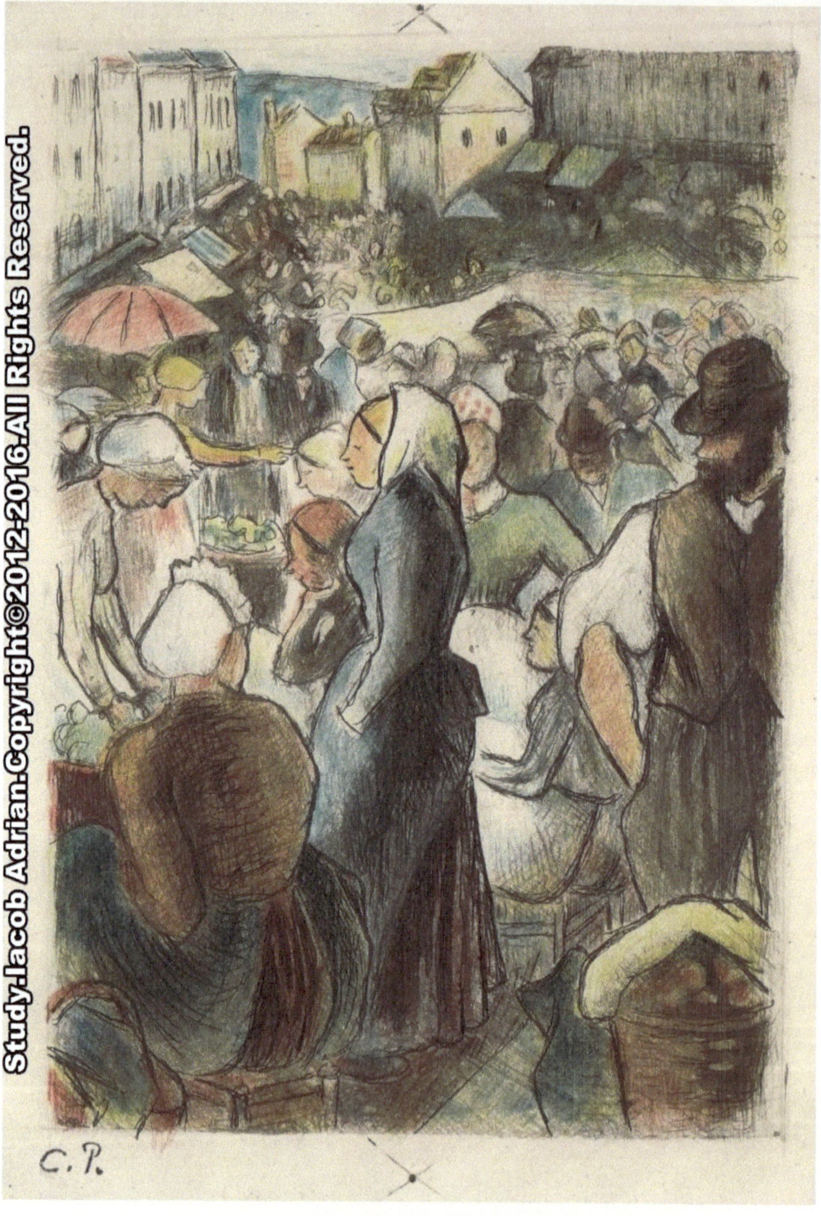

The Market at Gisors: Rue Cappeville
Date : 1894–1895

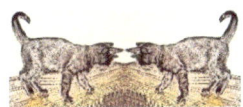

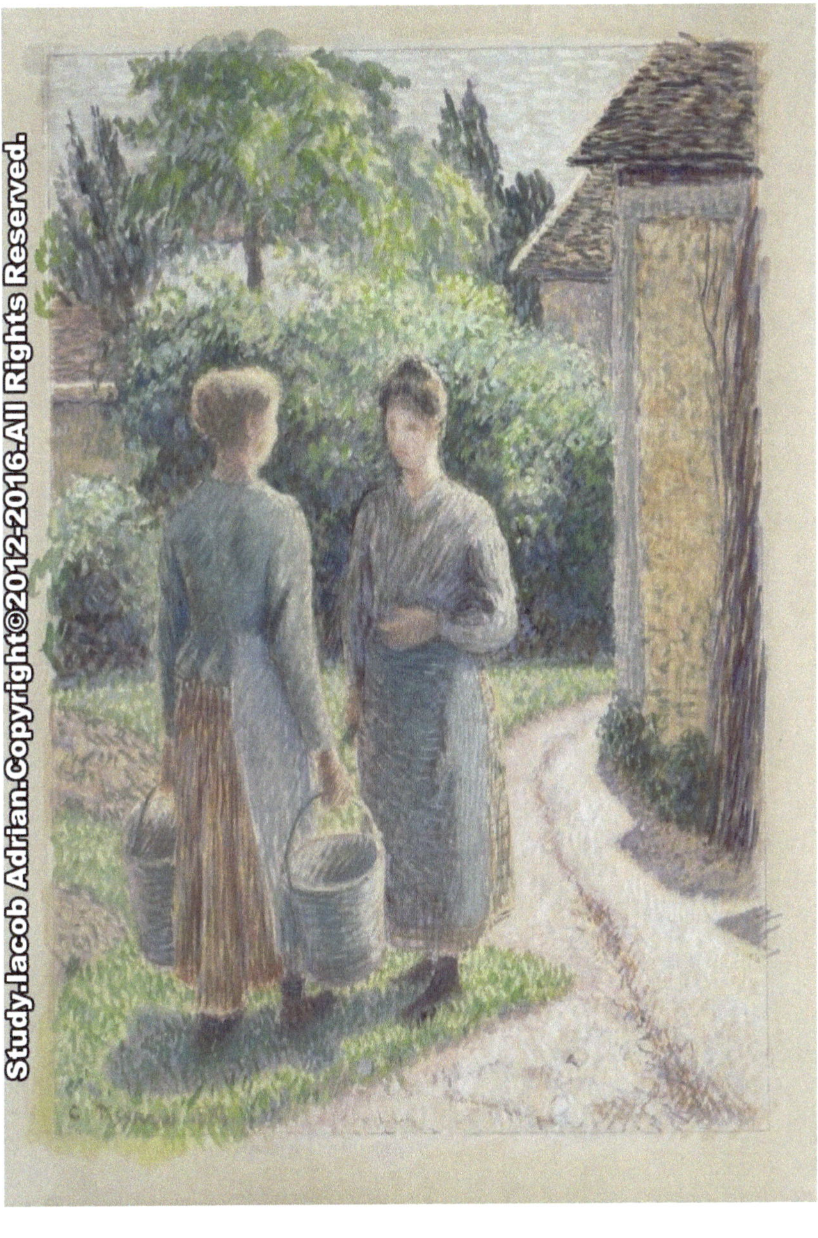

Two Women in a Garden
Date : 1888

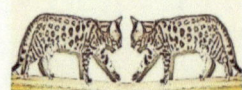

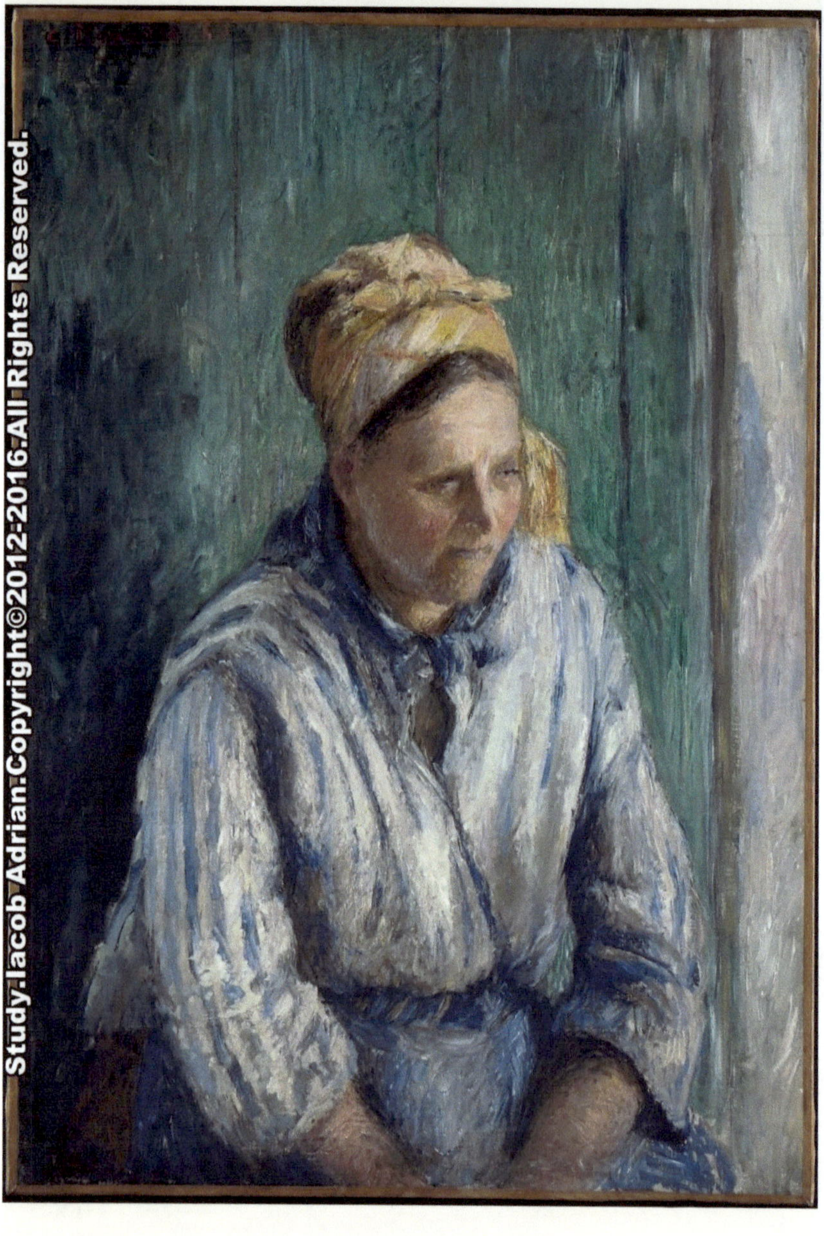

Washerwoman, Study
Date : 1860

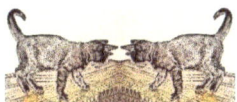

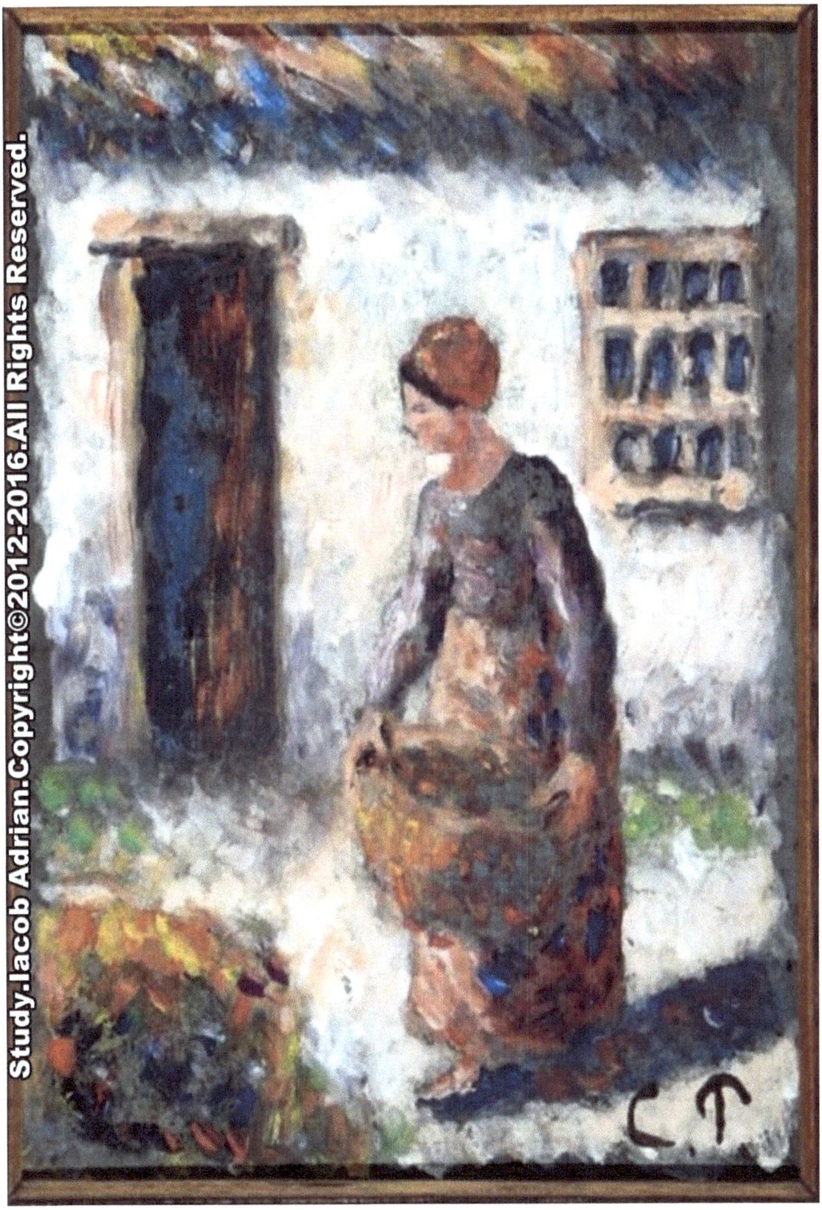

La paysanne à la manne
Date : 1895

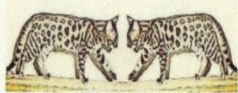

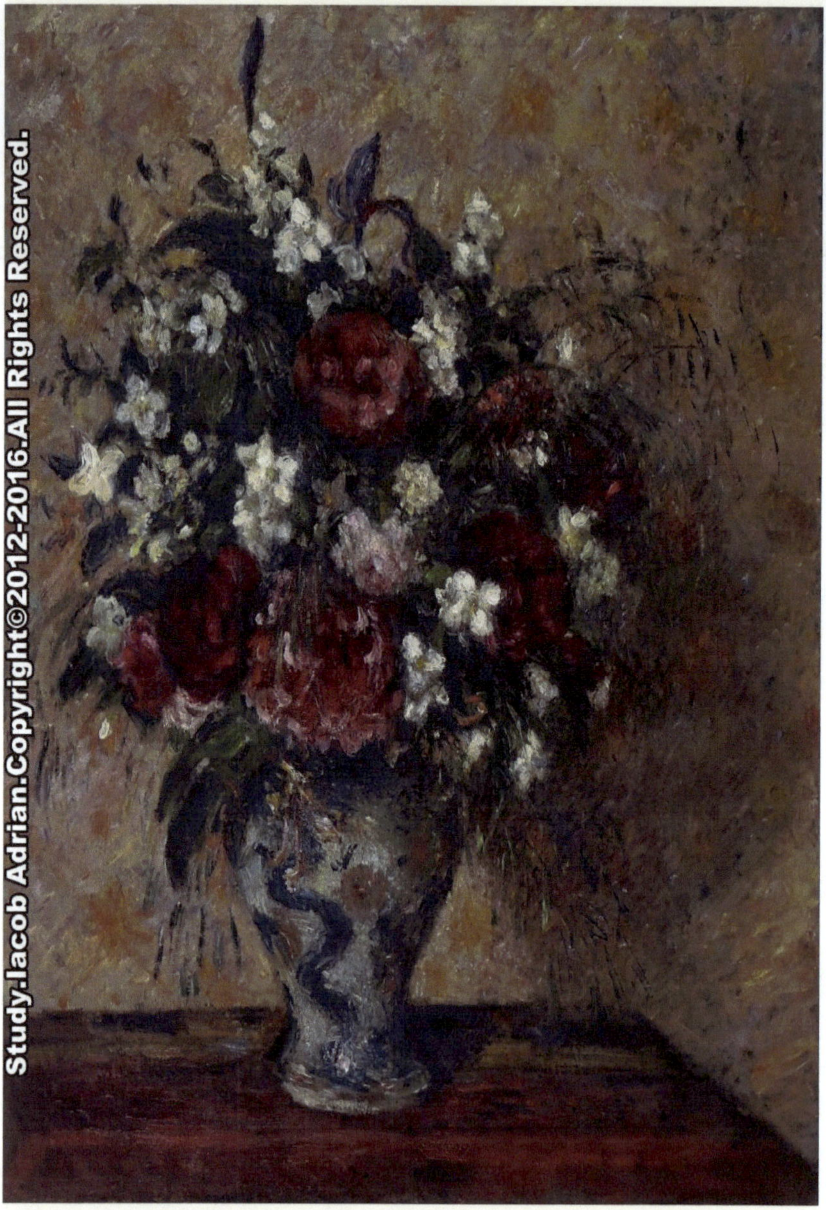

Still life with peonies and mock orange
Date : 1872 - 1877

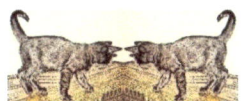

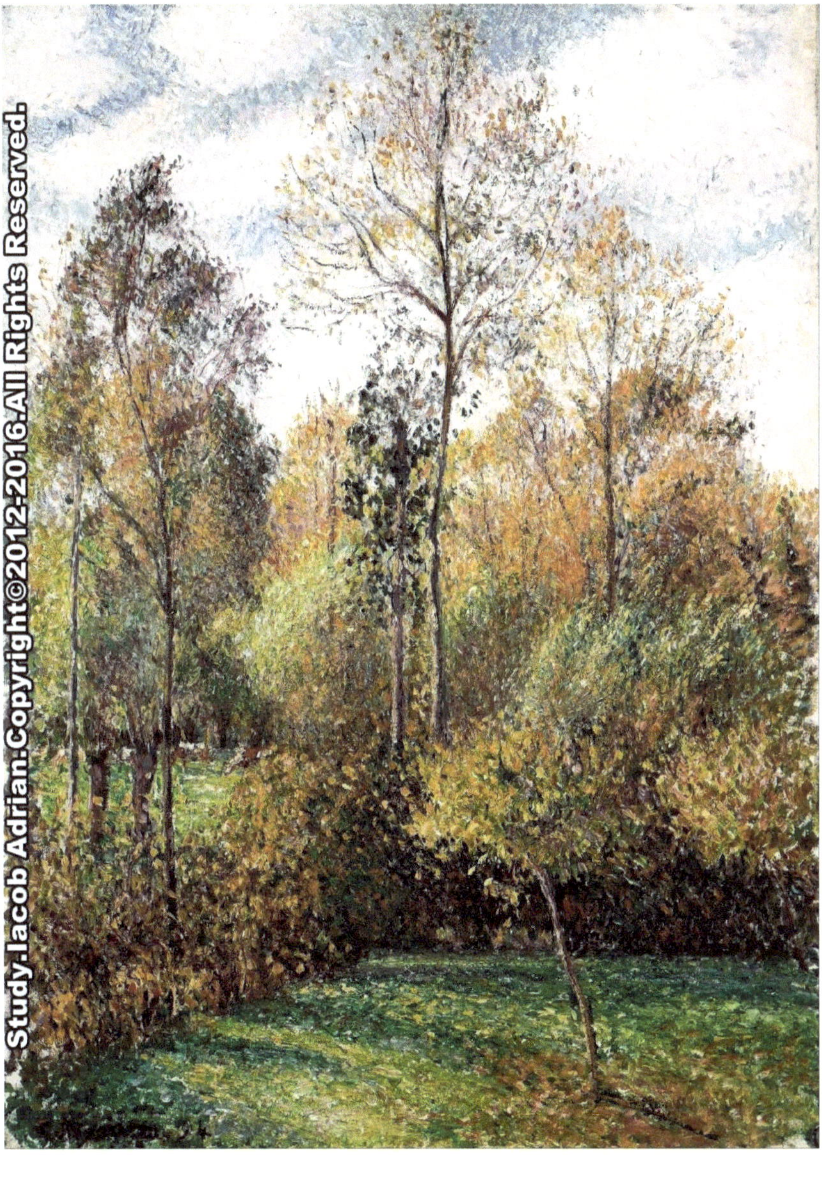

Automne, Peupliers, Eragny (Autumn, Poplars, Eragny)
Date 1894

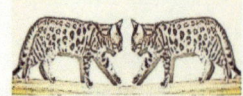

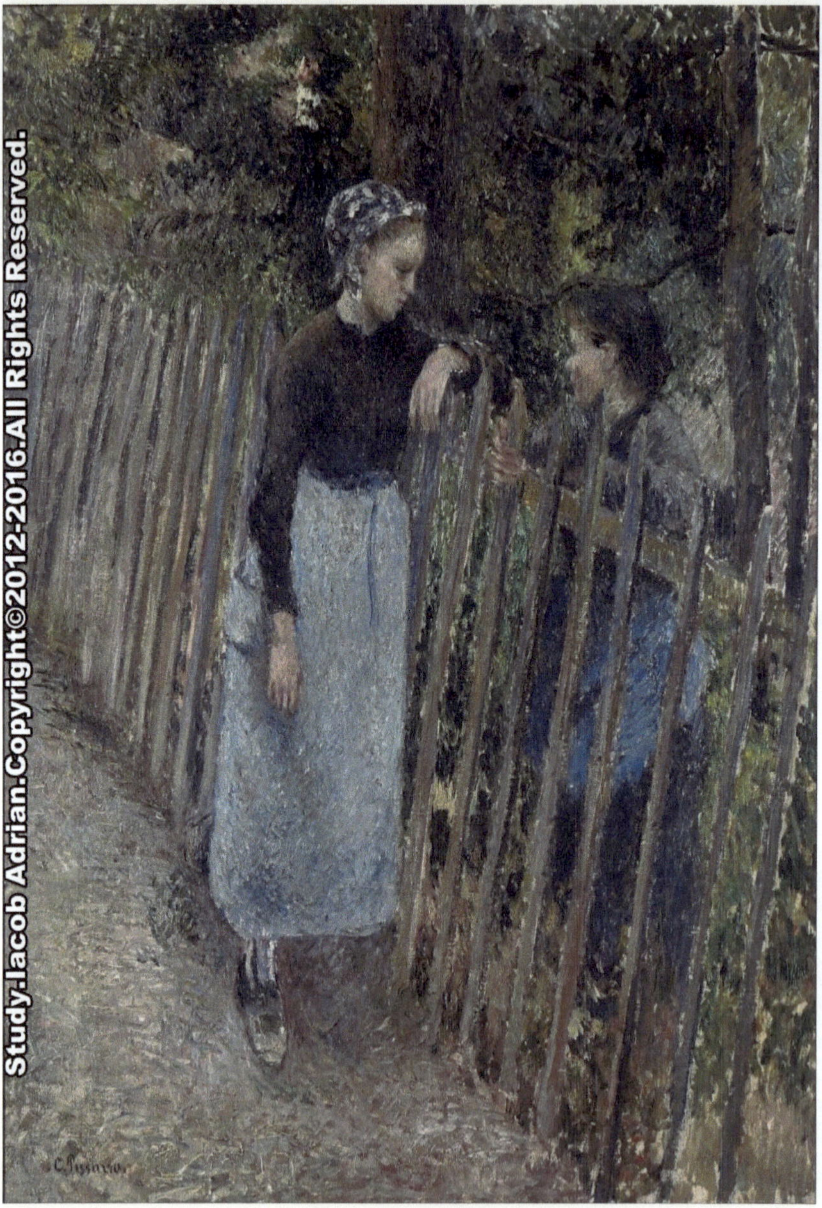

Conversation
Date : circa 1881

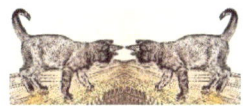

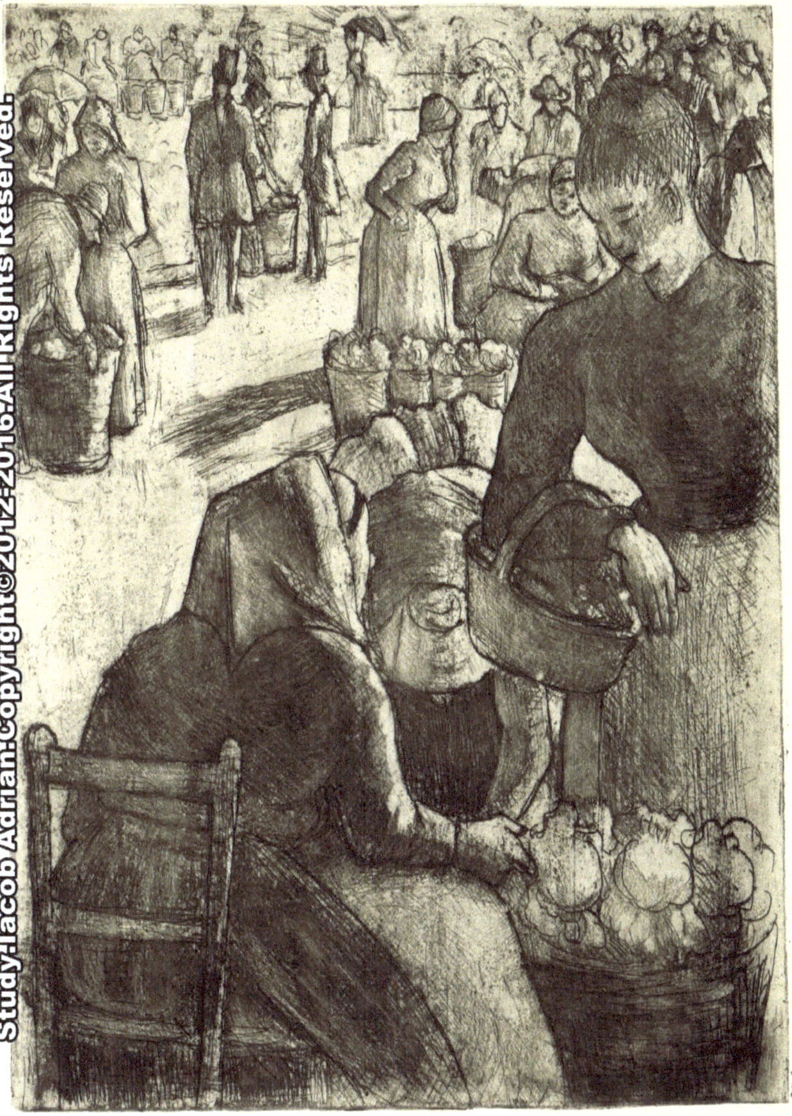

Marché aux Légumes à Pontoise
Date : 1891

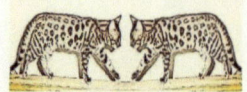

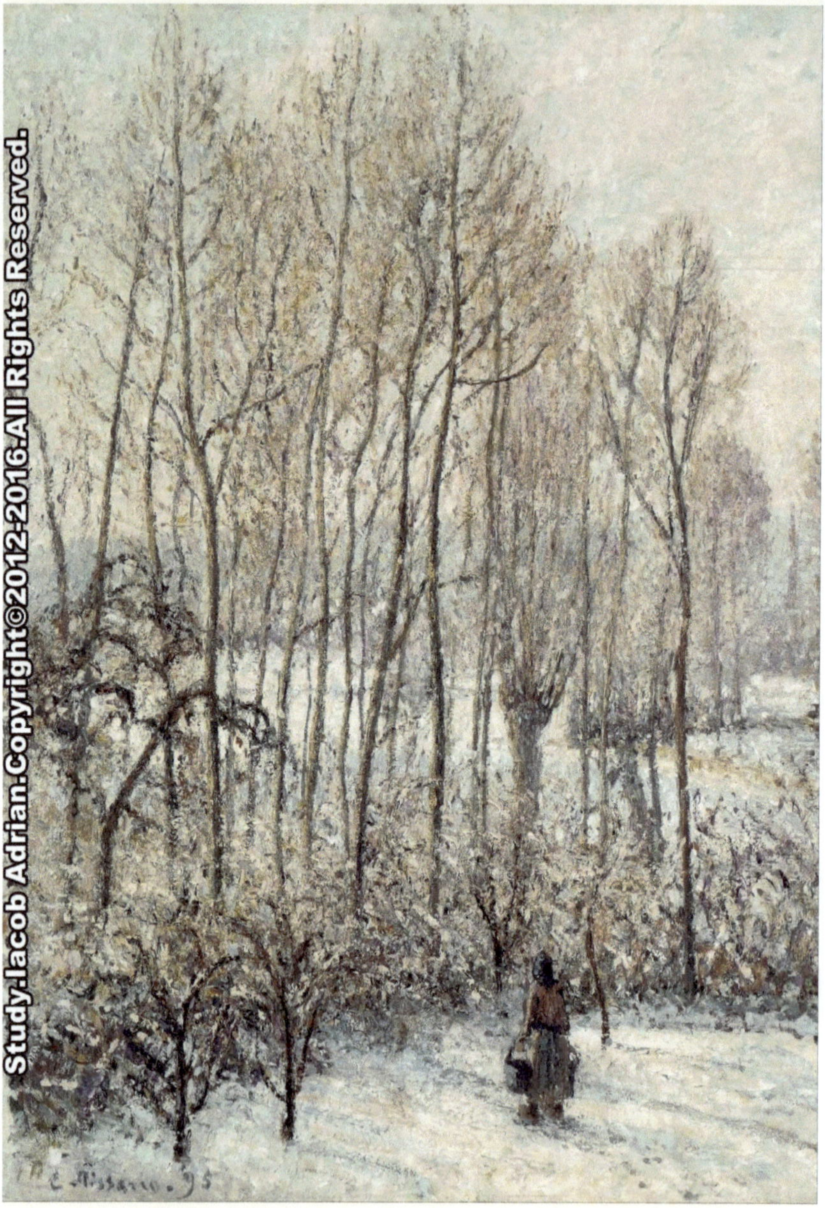

Morning Sunlight on the Snow, Eragny-sur-Epte
Date : 1895

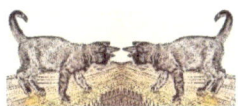

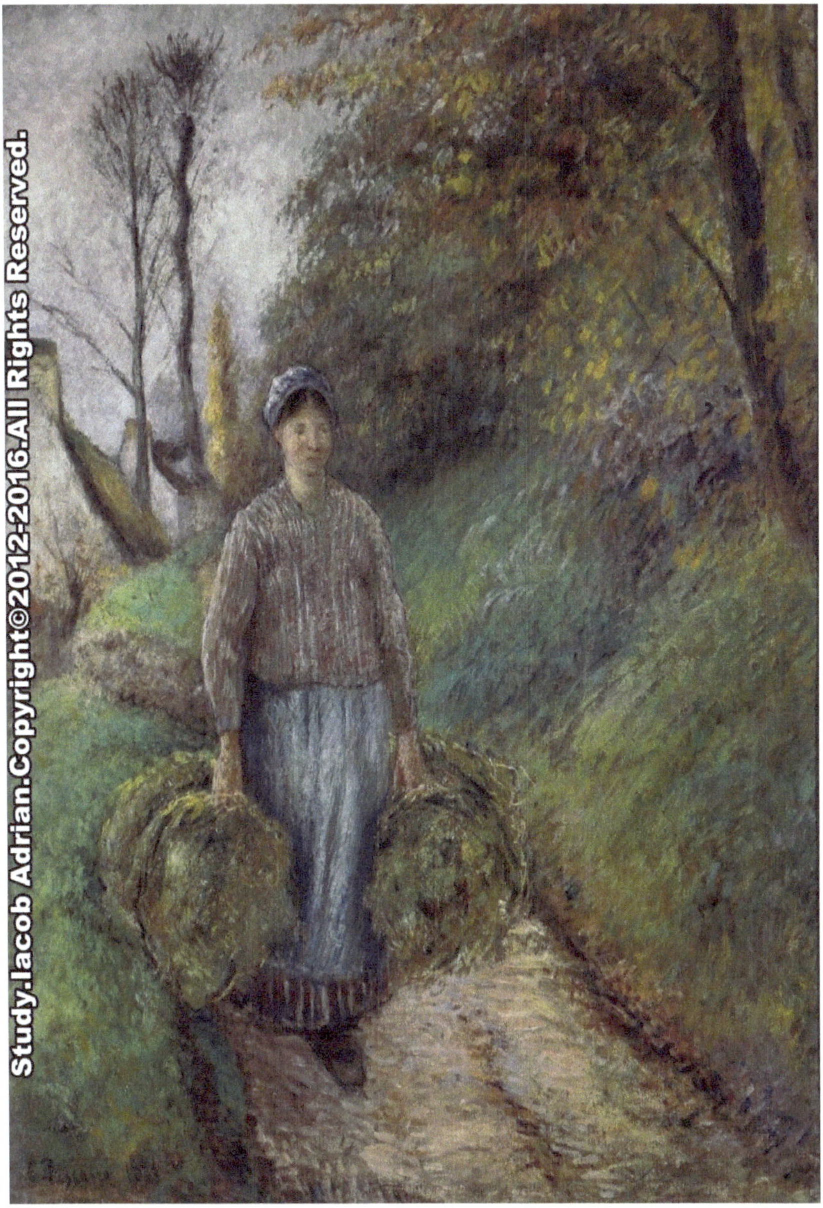

Peasant carrying two bales of hay
Date : 1883

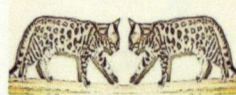

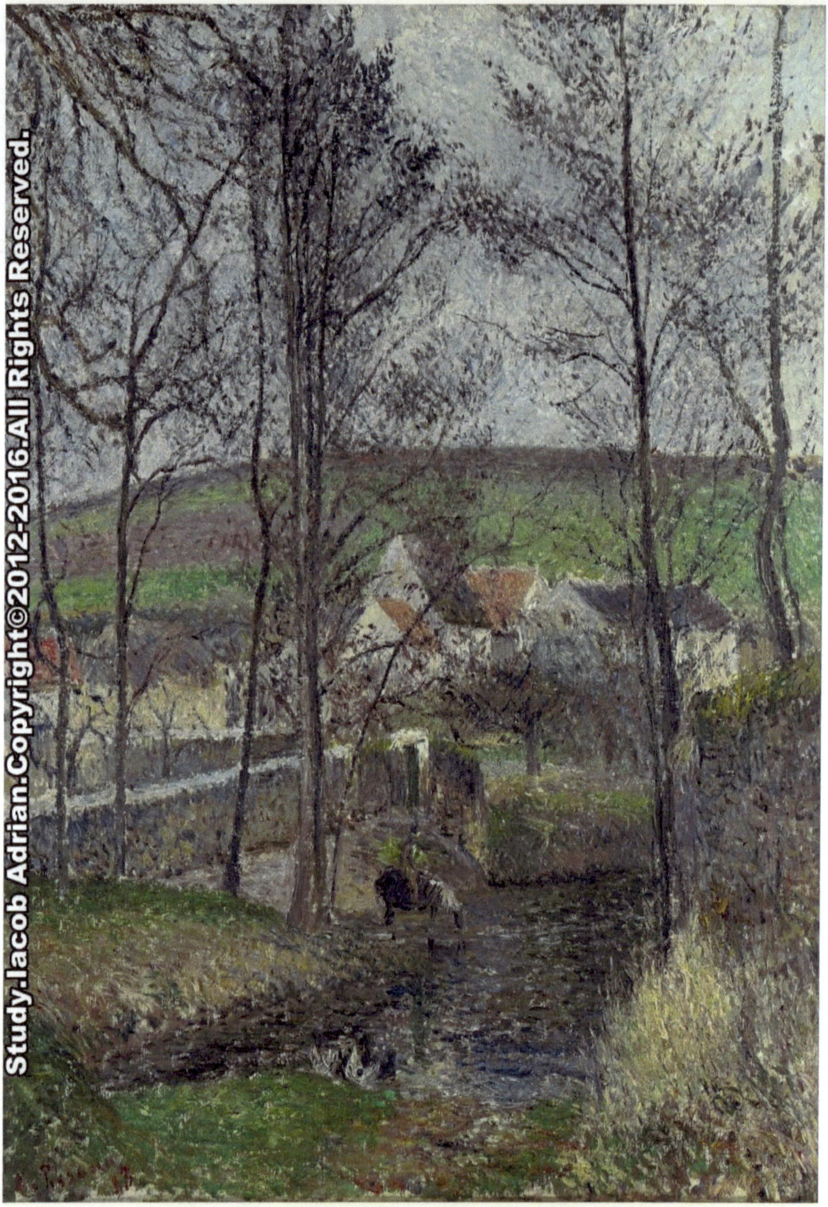

The banks of the Viosne at Osny
in grey weather, winter
Date : 1883

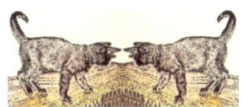

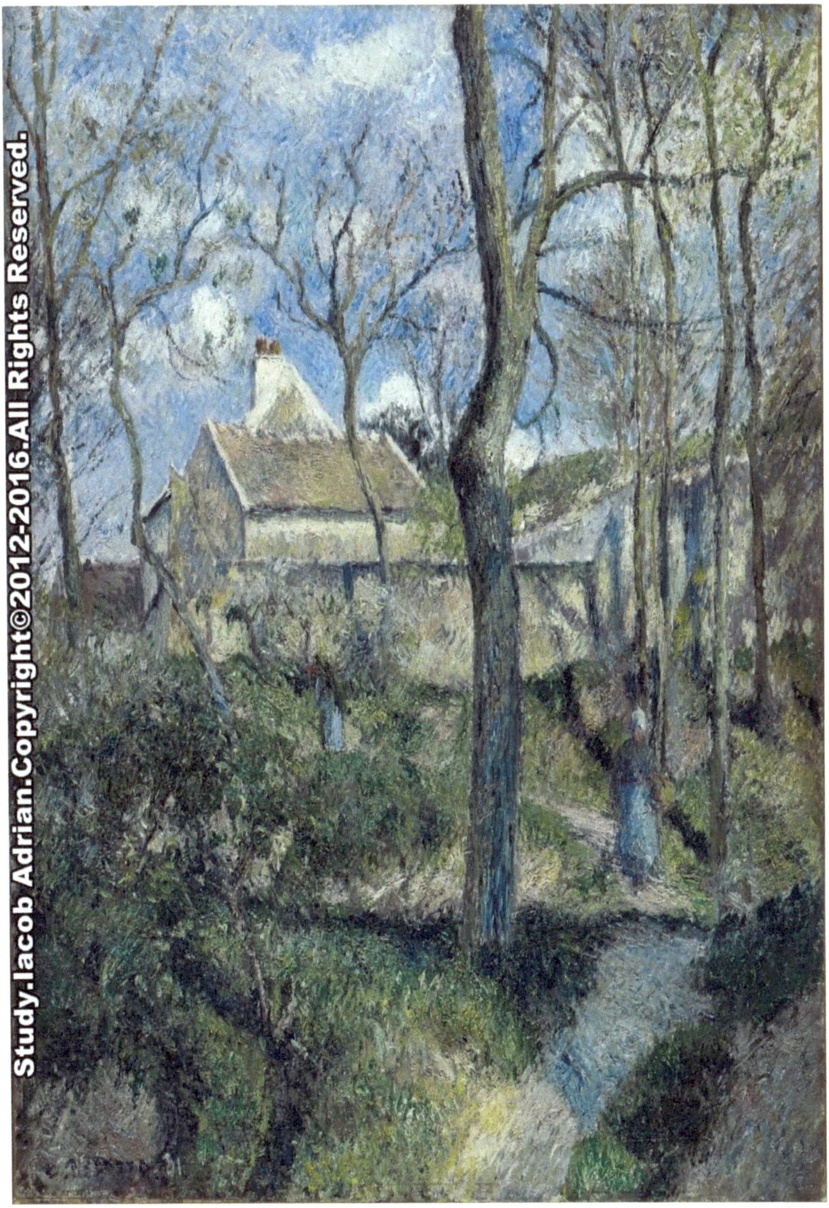

The Path to Les Pouilleux, Pontoise
Date : 1881

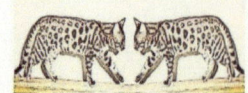

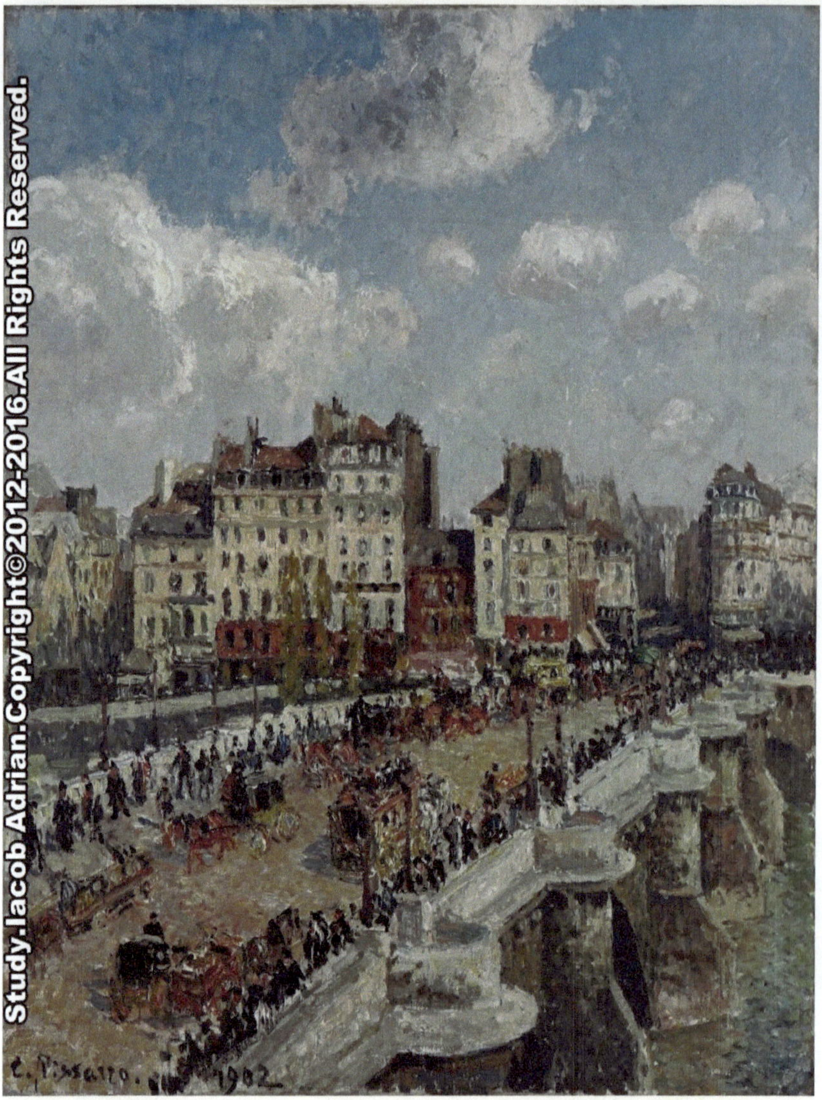

The Pont-Neuf
Date : circa 1902

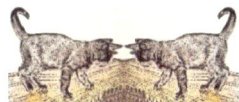

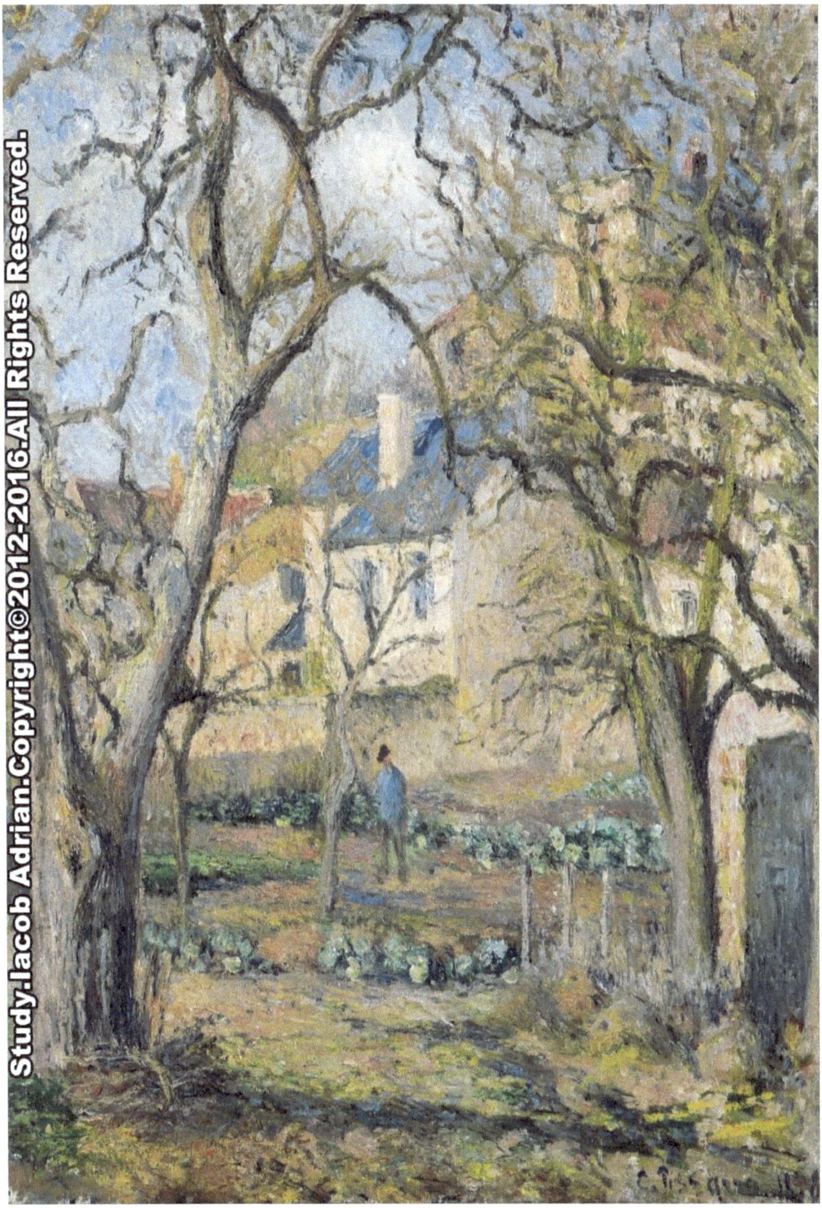

Vegetable Garden
Date : 1878

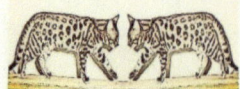

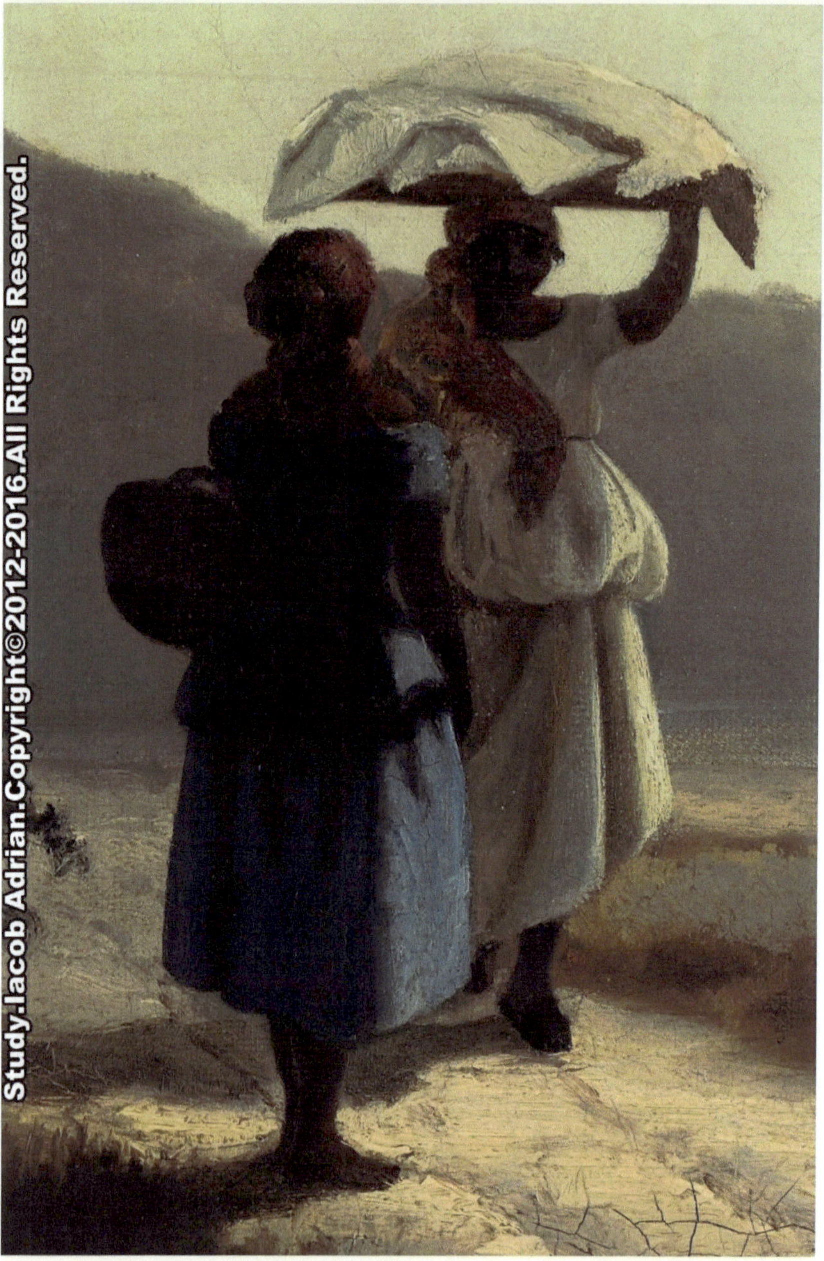

Two Women Chatting by the Sea, St. Thomas
Date : 1856

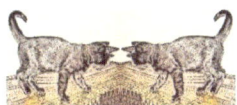

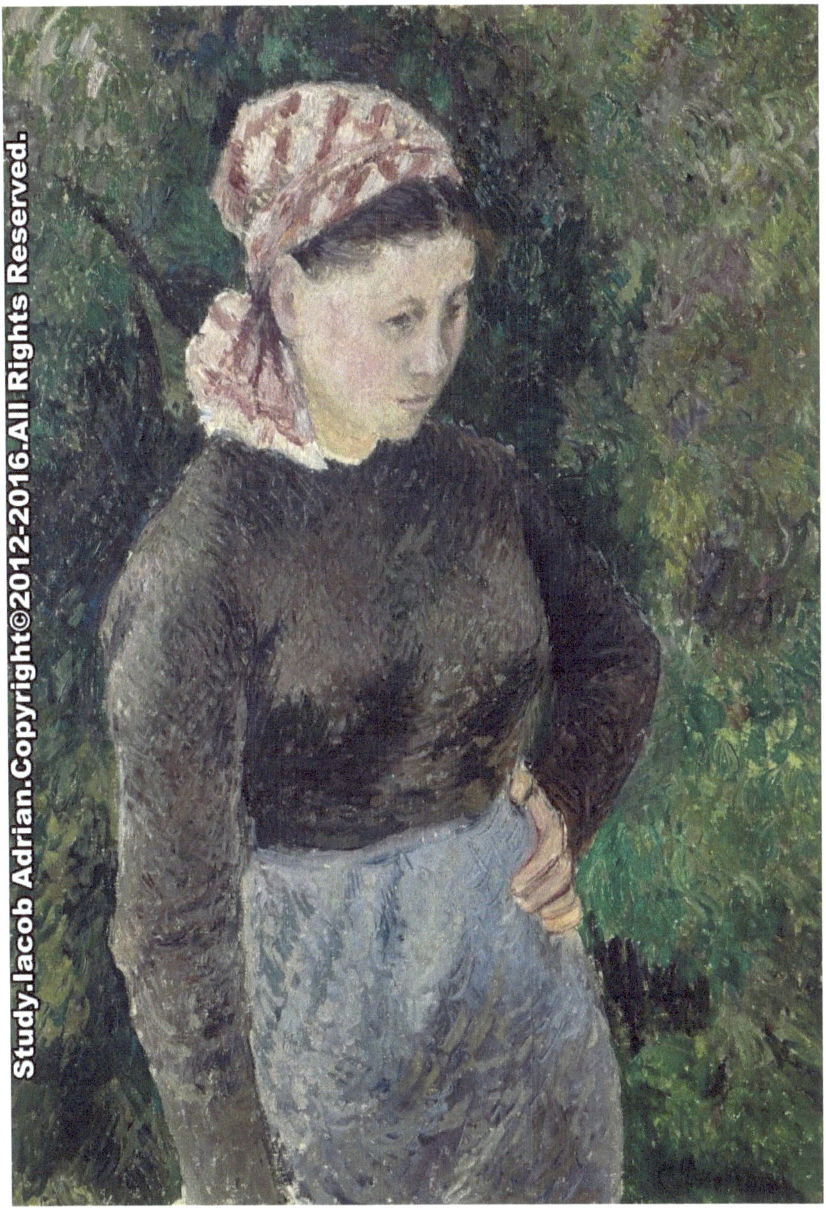

Peasant Woman
Date : 1880

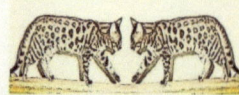

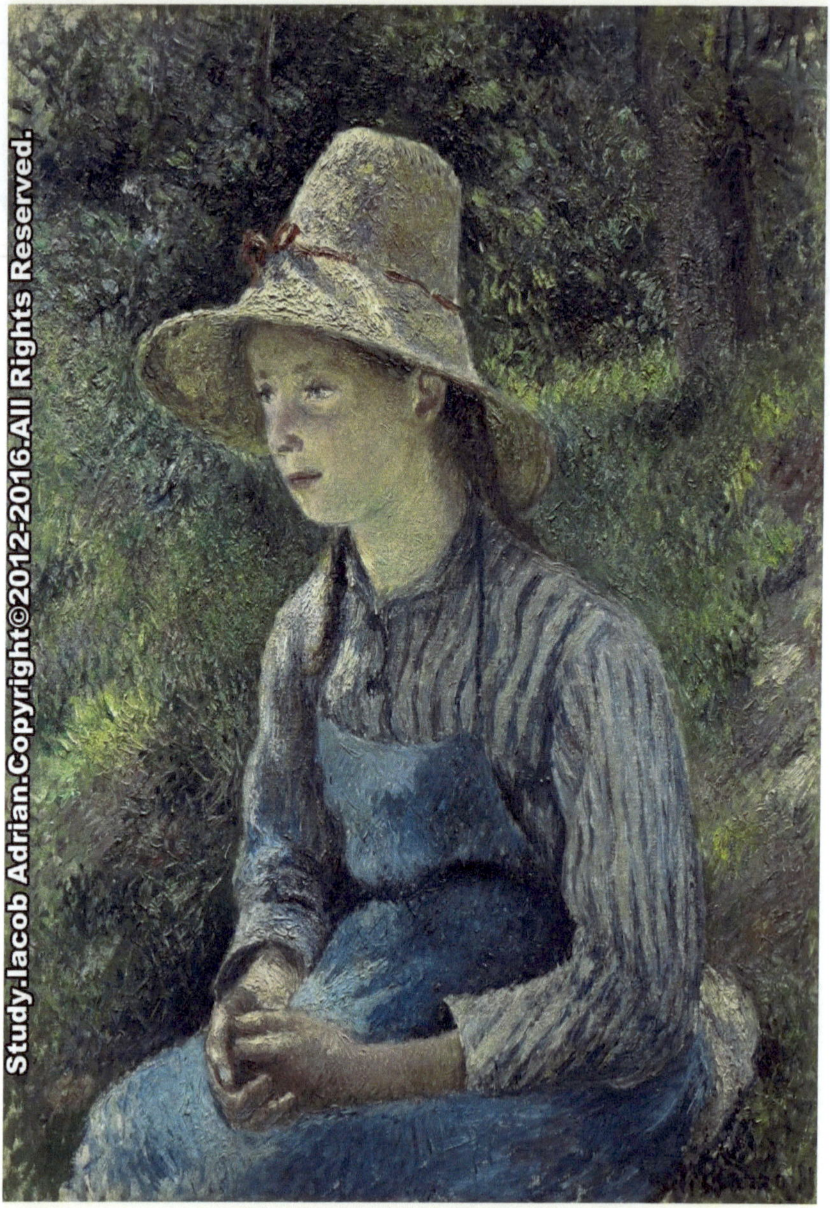

Peasant Girl with a Straw Hat
Date : 1881

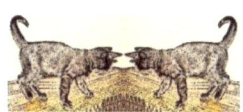

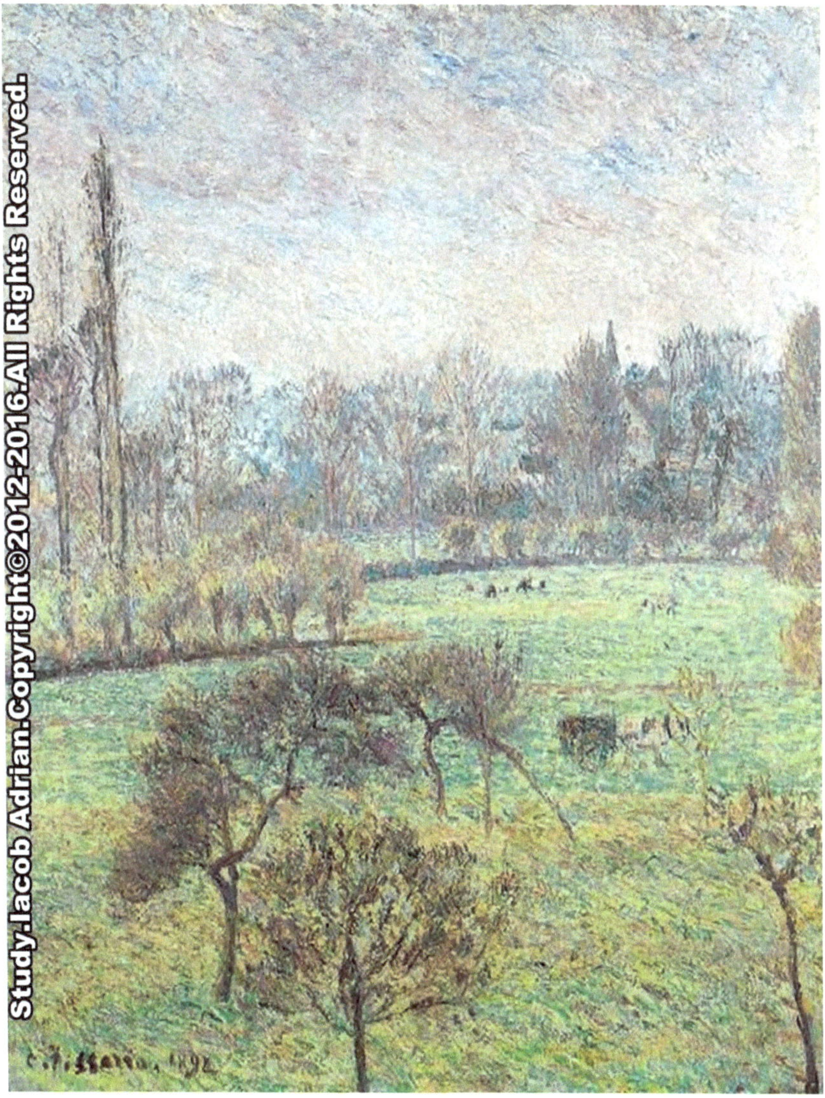

Matin, automne, Eragny
Date : 1892

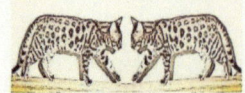

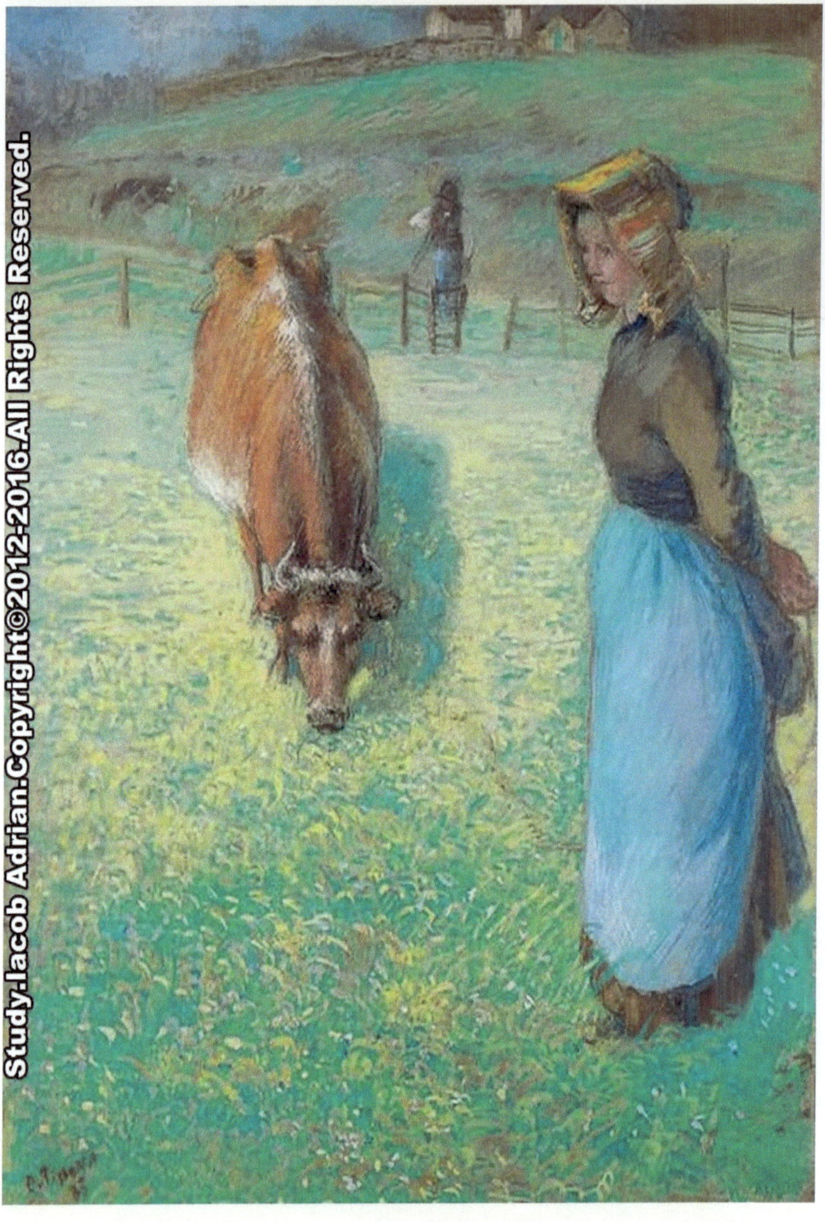

Paysanne gardant une vache, Osny
Date : 1883

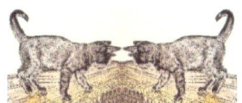

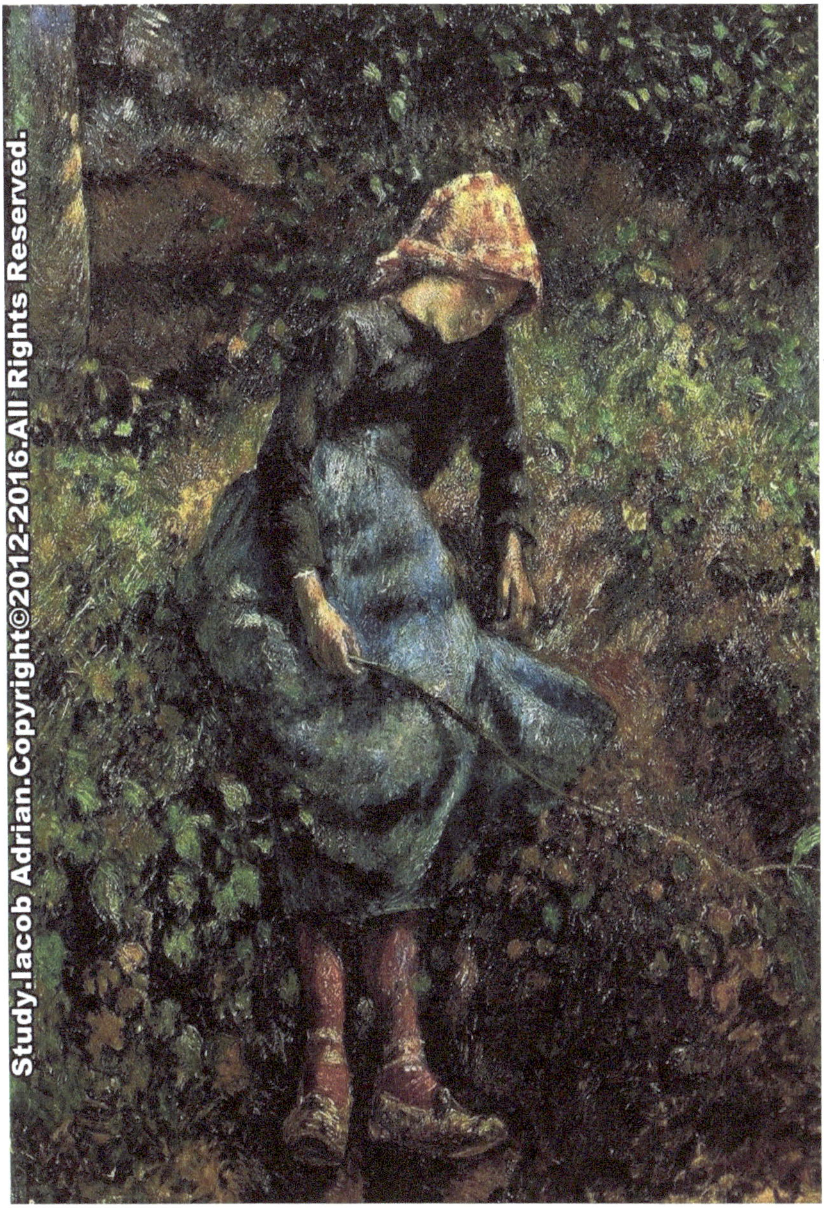

La bergère
Date : 1881

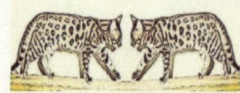

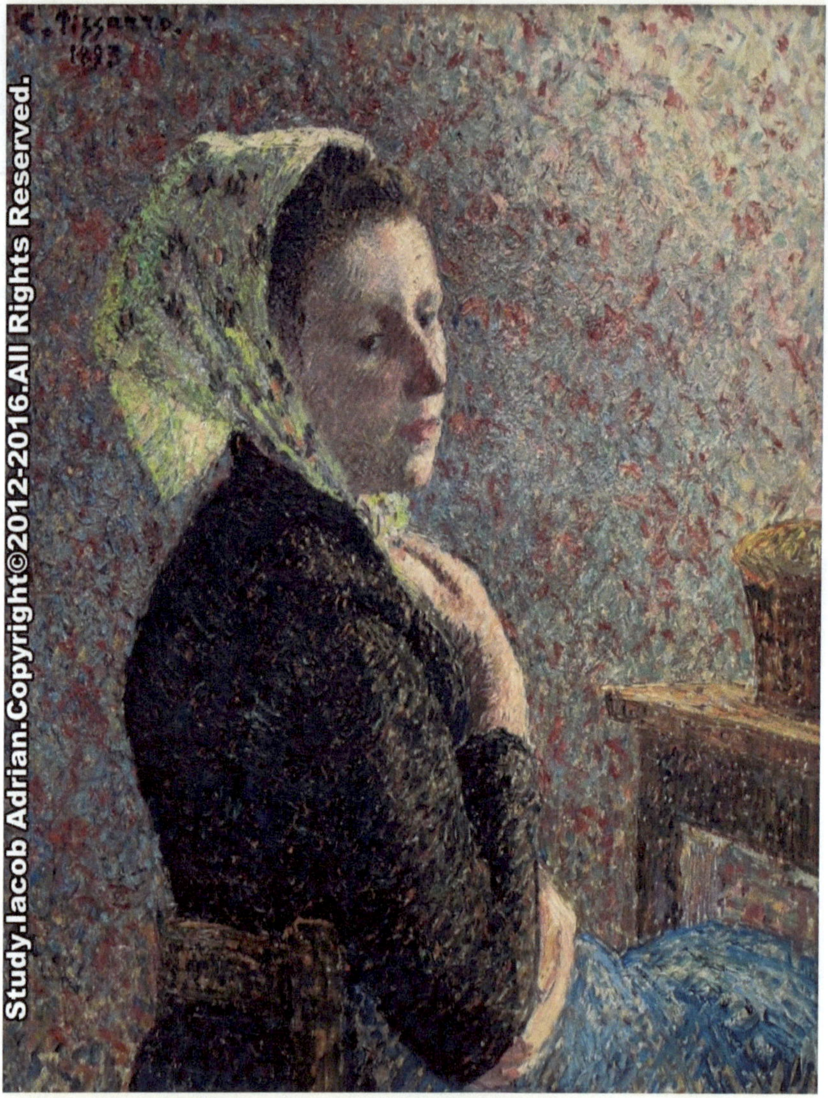

Woman with green scarf
Date : 1893

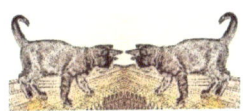

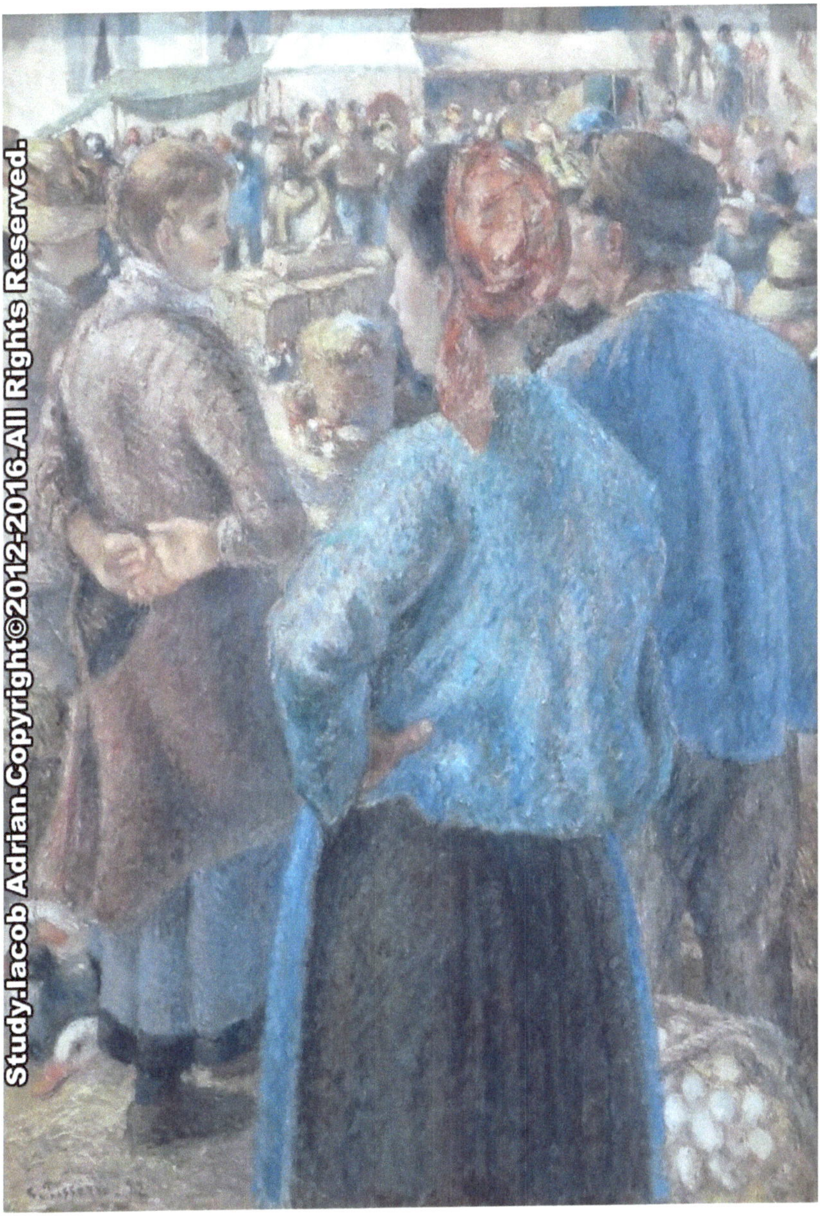

The Poultry Market, Pontoise
Date : 1882

Bibliographic sources :

Based on Paintings of
Camille Pissarro (1830-1903)

and

Materials and/or elements from :
- Documentary Studies 1 collection,
- Documentary Studies 4 collection,
- Iacob Images K 4.0 collection,
Author / owner of collections : Iacob Adrian

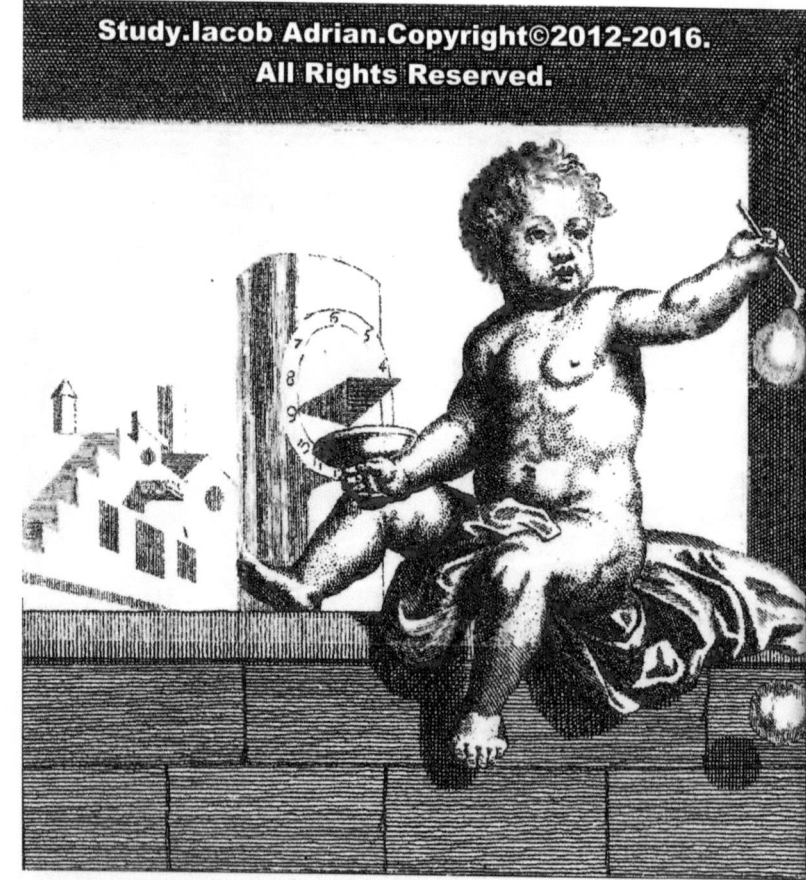

This documentary study use,
combined in various proportions,
elements from the following categories,
forms and subsets :
- fair use
- documentary
- documentary photography
- feature
- journalism
- arts journalism
- visual journalism
- photojournalism
- celebrity photography
in order to :
- employ material as the object of cultural critique ,
- quote to illustrate an argument or point ,
- use material in historical sequence,
providing independent opinion,
using photos, press articles, advertisements,
opinions of fans etc. ...

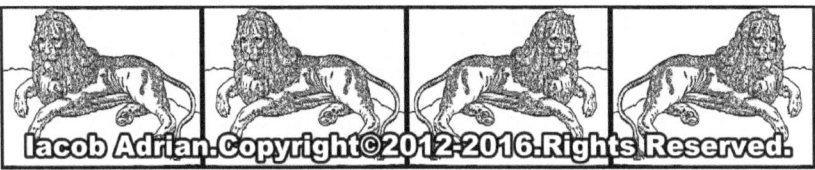

www.ingramcontent.com/pod-product-compliance
Lightning Source LLC
Chambersburg PA
CBHW040254220526
45473CB00001B/481